Frederick
from Alexandra
5/5/88

H. Casson

My First Colour Library

Telling the Time

The King's Clocks

Purnell

ISBN 0 361 03490 3

First published 1976 by Purnell Books, Paulton, Bristol BS18 5LQ, a member of the BPCC group
Made and printed in Great Britain by Purnell and Sons (Book Production) Limited Paulton, Bristol
Reprinted 1985
Written and illustrated by Ken Woodward

THE King was in a hurry again. Today he was in a hurry wherever he went. Now he was late for a meeting with some important visitors.

"I *do* wish the Jester was here," said the king to himself.

Several very important people were feeling most impatient.

They had been waiting for the King for *hours*.

"If only the King could learn to be on time," said a Prince to a Prime Minister, crossly.

Alone in the Royal Office, the King was worried and unhappy.

"I need my Jester," he sighed.

The Jester could tell the time properly, and the King relied on the Jester to tell *him* the time.

The Jester had been on a short holiday.

He returned to the palace the next day. It was mid-day, and the King was still in bed.

"Hello," said the King. "You know I need you to tell the time for me. Without you, I can't even set my alarm clock properly."

"The time has come for me to teach *you* how to tell the time, Your Majesty," smiled the Jester.

1

2

3

4

5

6

7

8

9

10

11

12

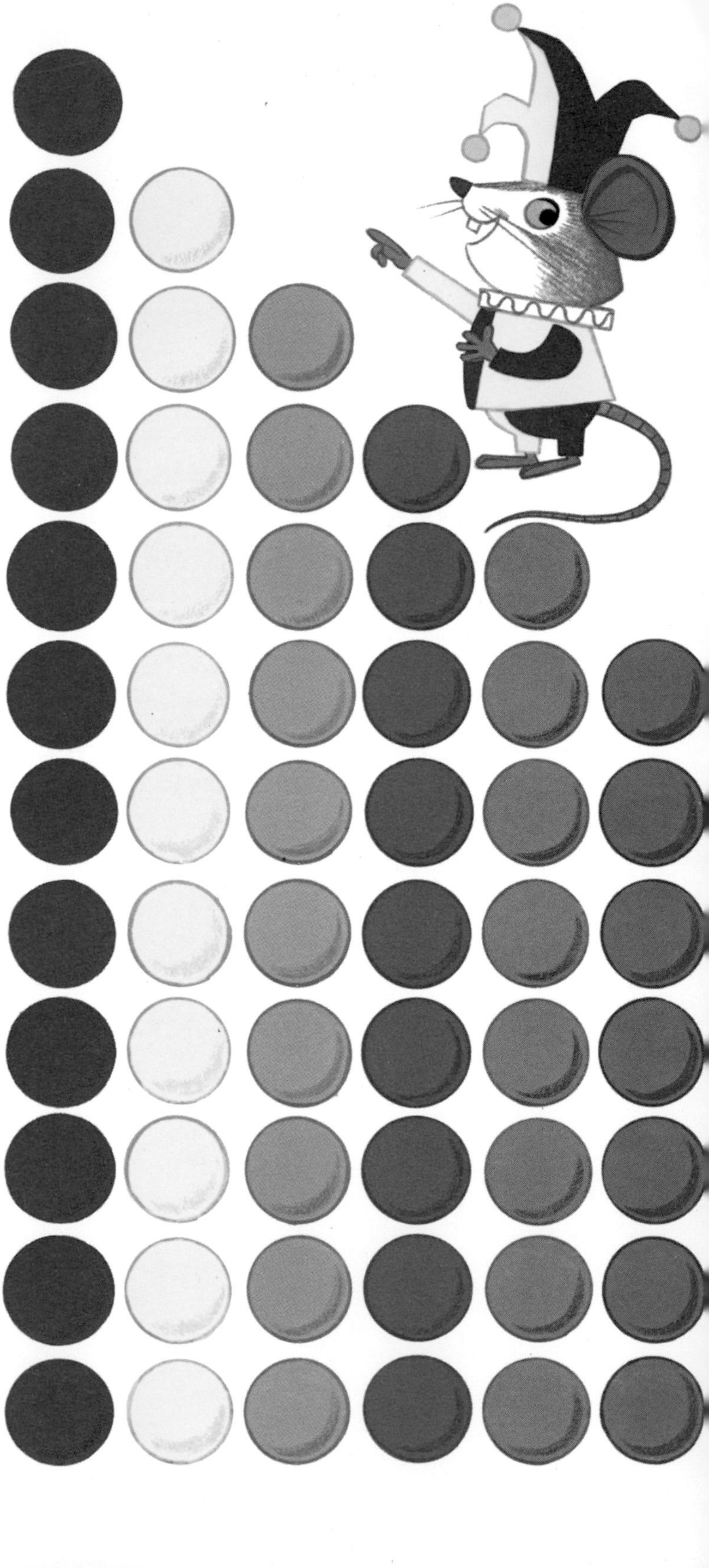

"To tell the time, first you must learn to count," the Jester told the King. This is the way the Jester helped the King to count.

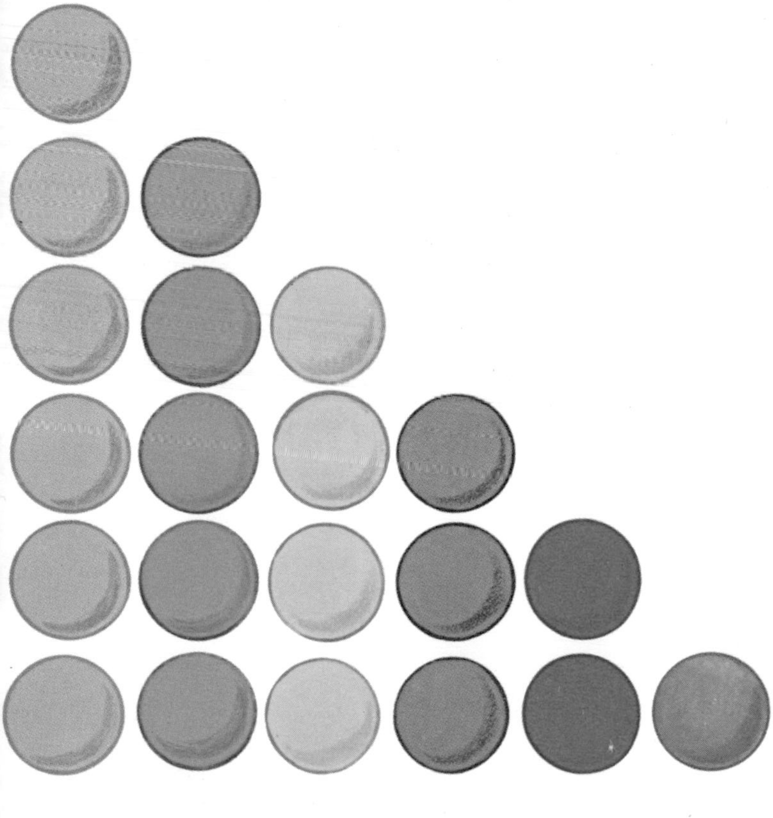

Everything was much better then. At one o'clock the King and the Jester played music. "This is the right time for the Royal Music," the Jester said.

The King felt so pleased.

At exactly two o'clock they went into the garden for the Royal Gardening. Today the King was going to do *everything* at the right time.

Three o'clock was Joke and Fun time.

At five o'clock the King and the Jester started to put on best Dinner Clothes.

"Dinner almost over by six o'clock? I like this," beamed the King. "I knew you would," said the Jester.

Then Cherry Pie was served.

The Jester asked the King if he wanted a quarter of the pie, or a half. "It's like a quarter of an hour, or a half an hour, Your Majesty," he said.

“I’ll have a quarter. This is a tasty way to learn about them.”

"There is something else you have to learn about clocks and telling the time," said the Jester. "Well, something extra to a quarter and a half."

This is a quarter past.

This is half-past.

This is a quarter to — the extra one!

Now the King could tell the time all the time.

The next morning the King started his new day so happily. "I'll not keep anyone waiting," he said.

The King hurried to the Royal Garage.
What time is it?

His Royal Friends were glad to meet him there.

Off went everyone in the Royal Red Car.
"We're going to the market," called the King.
He wanted to buy more clocks. The very best place to buy them was the market place. A clock man kept a stall there.
Can you see what time it is?

How pleasant it was, seeing the clocks that were for sale. The King bought quite a few. "We will take them to the palace, dear friends," he called.

The King bought his friends sweet cakes and drinks.

Then back to the palace they all went with the clocks.

Everyone helped the King unload the clocks, of course.

The King's clocks struck three o'clock.

The King and the Jester danced a clock-chime clog dance.